Bathrooms

PBC INTERNATIONAL, INC.

Bathrooms

BERNADETTE BACZYNSKI

JAMES W. KRENGEL, CKD, CBD, IIDA

Distributor to the book trade in the United States and Canada
Rizzoli International Publications through
St. Martin's Press, 175 Fifth Avenue, New York, NY 10010

Distributor to the art trade in the United States and Canada
PBC International, Inc., One School Street, Glen Cove, NY 11542

Distributor throughout the rest of the world
Hearst Books International, 1350 Avenue of the Americas, New York, NY 10019

Library of Congress Cataloging-in-Publication Data
Baczynski, Bernadette L.
Bathrooms / by Bernadette Baczynski.
p.   cm.
includes index
ISBN 0-86636-676-8 (hardcover). — ISBN 0-86636-677-6 (pbk.)
1. Bathrooms.   2. Interior decoration.   I. Title.
NK2117.B33B25 1998   98-9652
747.7'8—dc21   CIP

CAVEAT— Information in this text is believed accurate, and will pose no problem
for the student or casual reader. However, the author was often constrained by
information contained in signed release forms, information that could have been in
error or not included at all. Any misinformation (or lack of information) is the
result of failure in these attestations. The author has done whatever is possible to
insure accuracy.

10 9 8 7 6 5 4 3 2 1

Printed in Hong Kong

For my mother and for Aunt Mary,
with special thanks to my good friends
Barbara, Renée, Connie, and CJ.

BB

For my wife, Mary Lou, whose love, patience,
and understanding make it all worthwhile.

JK

Contents

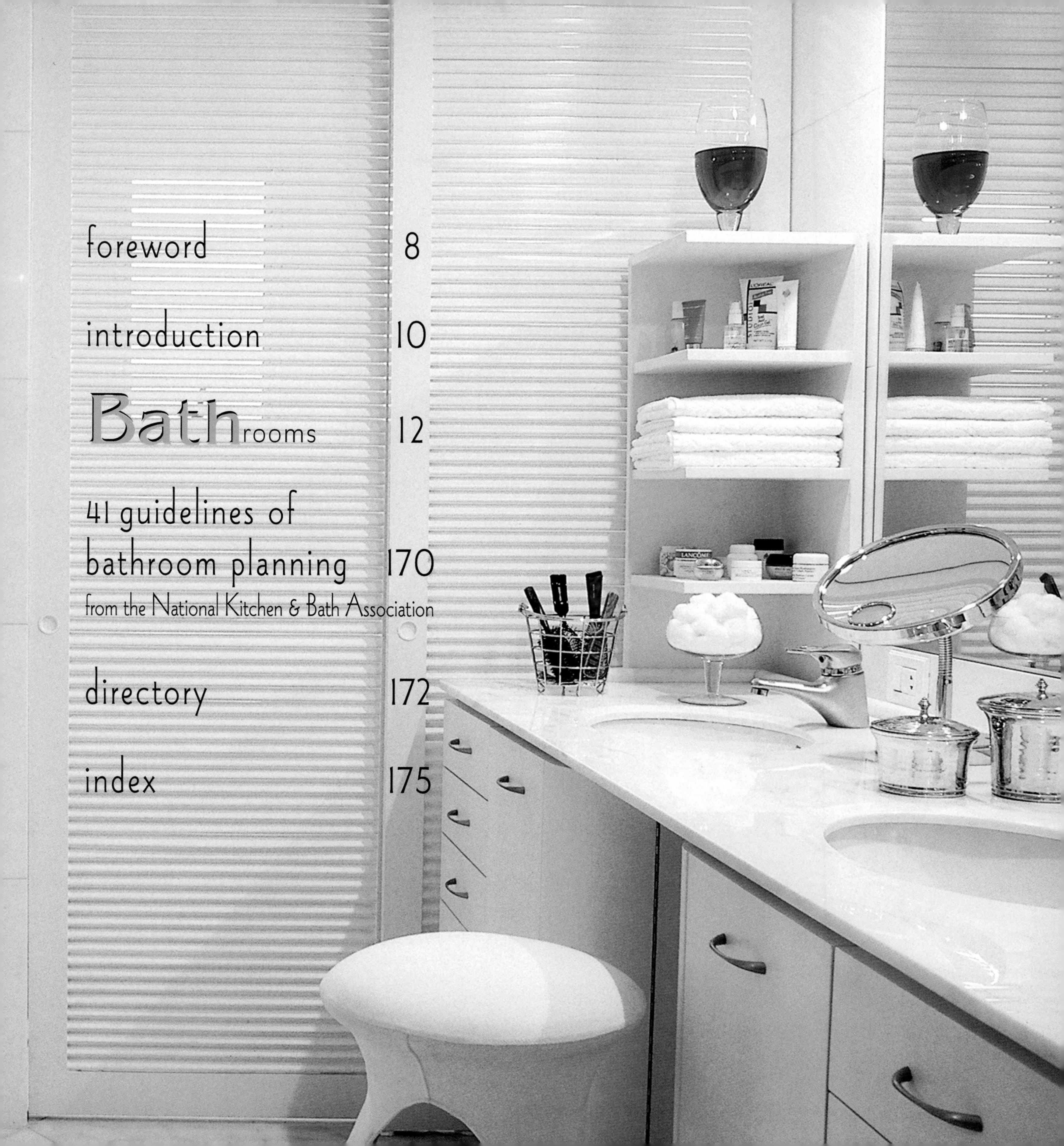

FOREWORD

The bathroom is in the midst of a renaissance. Spaces, both large and small, are now enriched with luxurious materials, fine furnishings and unexpected details. Design is of paramount importance and limited only by imagination. Choices abound on a continuum between classic traditional and the sleek lines of contemporary design.

These fresh designs result directly from the increased functions today's bathroom serves. Master baths have evolved into intimate retreats to which homeowners escape to pamper themselves and relieve the tension of day-to-day life. Likewise, the powder room has become the "jewel box" of the home, a small space homeowners can transform into a miniature gallery of self-expression.

Present-day consumers demand unique, functional bathrooms that are extensions of their personalities. Design advancements are meeting these demands, elevating the bathroom's luxury and graciousness to a new level. New textural surface treatments, striking above-counter lavatories and sumptuous whirlpools with hydro-massage technology are just a few of the innovations the industry has seen in recent years.

Looking to the millennium and beyond, the bathroom will continue to develop as a retreat for both pampering and personal expression. As the pressures and stresses of daily life continue to mount, people will increasingly turn to bathrooms that reflect their individuality——places that are truly their own.

Laura Kohler, Vice President-Communications

KOHLER.

INTRODUCTION

In recent years, bath design has come into its own. No longer uninspired, strictly utilitarian rooms, today's bathrooms are an integral part of a home's style and character.

Like the bedroom or den, today's bathroom is a private place in which to relax and refocus. For some busy families, baths may be communal gathering rooms. For others, baths are secluded, tranquil retreats. Some baths are cozy havens amid busy surroundings; others are open and light, making the outdoors an integral, defining element in their design.

The bathrooms shown in this book represent the efforts of interior designers and architects from around the world. Working within the requirements of their clients and the spaces themselves, these professionals have taken bath design to new levels and, in the process, contributed to an extraordinary wealth of fine design internationally. As you review their work, you'll appreciate their innovative responses to each challenge and find new inspiration for your own creative spirit.

Bernadette Baczynski
James W. Krengel, CKD, CBD, IIDA

10

ESSENTIALLY AESTHETIC

In this bathroom, designed for a young European couple, "functional needs are met in such a way that their essential forms become aesthetic qualities," says Italian architect and designer Livia Tomiselli. "Each material is allowed to express its nature without complicated details."

Tomiselli's philosophy is in accord with the home's sleek '60s nature. Situated with expansive views of city and ocean, the house is a study in natural light and spatial continuity that blends its interior with the outdoors. The master bath, lacking exterior walls or windows, has been excluded from this openness.

Tomiselli's redesign gives the new master bath a clean, somewhat aquatic feel, making "every element essential and almost nonexistent." Natural light now streams in from a skylight, and expansive panels of sandblasted glass separate the bath from the bedroom corridor without blocking light. White Carrara marble, veined with gray-green striations, blends with the aqua glass counter. A gently mottled mix of glass mosaic tiles captures the feeling of sea and sky. On the vanity, chrome accessories and fixtures illustrate Tomiselli's premise that essentials can indeed be aesthetic elements.

ARCHITECT/INTERIOR DESIGNER: Tomarch Interior Design
LOCATION: Brentwood, California   DESIGN BUDGET: $30,000   SQUARE FEET/METERS: 105/10
PHOTOGRAPHY: Derek Rath

Previous Spread The skylight, the room's new source of natural light, is visible above the tub. A sliding door and wall of sandblasted glass separate the bath from the master bedroom corridor.

Left To create a visual separation in the room, Tomiselli designed a sleek birch-and-glass cabinet, which seems suspended in mid-air by simple chrome tubes.

Right The curvilinear mirror offsets the austerity of the room's other elements. Its shape represents a cloud. The four lights inserted in it depict the moon, the planet, the sun, and the star.

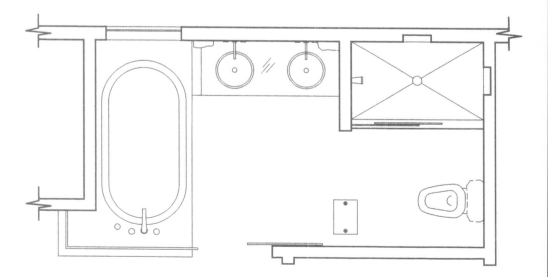

AN INTEGRATED VISION

o create a sense of privacy and still take full advantage of the desert view," says architect Bil Taylor, "I imagined a mountain pool in a quiet setting, then designed an abstract image of that concept." The results of his vision are a home and master bath completely in harmony with their surroundings, a seamless blend of external and internal environments.

The centerpiece of this bath, created for a professional couple, is a cast-in-place concrete tub. Its color and material are an extension of the concrete floors used throughout the house. The room's sleek, hard surfaces are softened not only by a palette of natural tones, but by the unique way those tones are introduced into the design: color in both concrete and wall plaster is integral to the materials, giving surfaces an unusual depth and subtle variation. Oak cabinets are washed. Natural light filters in through a series of skylights.

To tame the view of the Arizona landscape, Taylor framed a vignette of the scene in a doorway, connecting indoor and outdoor spaces by means of a private patio. "It's an environmentally sensitive room," says Taylor, "futuristic yet respectful of its timeless setting."

ARCHITECT: Bil Taylor Design Associates   INTERIOR DESIGNER: Dean Ladas
LOCATION: Tucson, Arizona   DESIGN BUDGET: not disclosed   SQUARE FEET/METERS: 250/23
PHOTOGRAPHY: Ray Allbright Photography

Previous Spreads From the private patio, sunbathers have unobstructed access to the shower. To unify the spacious bathing area, the floor and walls are faced with individually selected slate tiles. A single ledge is incorporated into the tub surround for ease of access as well as extra towel storage. The cool colors of the slate also create a dramatic gallery wall for art works from the couple's collection.

Above Matte-finished ceramic tiles on the tub's interior repeat the hues and variations of slate tiles on the wall. A tiled inset on the tub surround accents the faucet.

Right Through louvered double doors, a spacious laundry room adjoins her vanity and the master bedroom closet to the right. The doorway-height mirror separates the vanity and shower areas, allowing both spaces to share natural light.

Opposite A privacy wall divides his vanity from the water closet alcove. The area is illuminated by a series of skylights.

SHARING THE WARMTH

In this newly created master suite, a fireplace that's visible from both bath and bedroom is a key architectural element, says architect Larry Bogdanow. That, along with three generous windows and French doors opening onto the bedroom, have turned a once-tiny bathroom into an airy and light-filled space.

For the busy professional parents who share the bathroom, a calm, soothing environment was essential. "Our aesthetic choices support that requirement," says Bogdanow. A palette of warm, creamy beiges sets the room's mood. Built-in luxuries such as the fireplace, whirlpool, and marble and limestone surfaces are enriched by the luxury of abundant natural light. The room is also rich in subtle details, especially in the various applications and patterns of tumbled marble tiles. Because the room is spacious, mirrors are used simply and sparingly: a pine-framed mirror rests atop the mantel, another is framed in tile by the vanity, and a small, wall-mounted makeup mirror serves both vanity and dressing table.

ARCHITECT/INTERIOR DESIGNER: Bogdanow Partners Architects PC
LOCATION: Montclair, New Jersey   DESIGN BUDGET: $38,000   SQUARE FEET/METERS: 300/28
PHOTOGRAPHY: Reprinted with permission from House Beautiful Kitchens/Baths.
Copyright 1997 The Hearst Corp. Photo by: Mark Samu

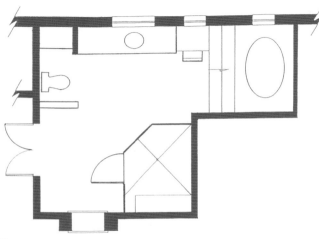

Previous Spread A fireplace is visible in bedroom and bath, its tumbled marble mantelpiece mirroring the design in the shower stall. French doors of whitewashed pine blend into the soft earth tones of the limestone and marble.

Above Turn-of-the-century reproduction hardware adorns the marble-topped vanity which is centered below an elegant arched window. A lowered marble counter between the vanity and tub serves as a dressing table.

Right Two steps lead to the whirlpool tub. The window above the tumbled-marble pattern opens onto those in the stairwell behind it, allowing an exchange of light between spaces.

REBIRTH OF POMPEII

"My desire to capture an idealized reality took me to Pompeii, the inspiration for this stylized master bathroom," says designer Chris Nicole Prince. Created for the Cancer Research Institute Show House, the bath is the ultimate escape, an exploration of an ancient theme that is skillfully integrated into a modern context, evocative yet entirely functional.

The room reflects Prince's love of natural materials, "the most tactile," whose use and look she explores by acid-washing surfaces and leaving edges unfinished, as if they had just been taken from a quarry. On the floor, stone pavers were placed randomly into cement, which was stained and raked to imitate dried mud. Surfaces are pitted, edges left rough or broken, reinforcing the room's look of antiquity. The ceiling was softly faux-painted to resemble clouds and sky. Bringing the room back to the present, pieces of 20th-century artwork juxtapose with its ancient theme, adding unexpected contemporary touches.

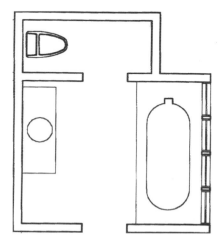

"It's a sensuous, harmonious room with an exciting point of view," says Prince, "rooted in the past yet decidedly a part of the present moment."

INTERIOR DESIGNER: Simon's Hardware & Bath
LOCATION: New York, New York   DESIGN BUDGET: $85,000   SQUARE FEET/METERS: 250/23
PHOTOGRAPHY: Tim Lee Photography

A Roman keystone arch separates the water closet from the main bath, leaving visible a glazed, wallpapered niche to display an antique African chair. To heighten the feeling of an archaeological excavation, some floor tiles were deliberately broken or left out of the pattern. Surrounding the unrestored 19th-century frame, custom copper-and-onyx sconces illuminate the area.

THE NESTING INSTINCT

ike a nest of boxes, this cleverly constructed master bath reveals itself in layers. "It was designed as a box within a box," says architect Ken Rorrison of this room for the busy parents of two. "We used the space between the existing shell and the new panels to hide utilities and irregularities, and to create storage areas."

The bath's collage of squares and rectangles is much more than homage to a Mondrian canvas: the brightly colored panels indicate storage and cupboard spaces; beige panels are extensions of existing walls; birch panels conceal utilities. Glass mosaic tiles in blue dominate the palette, suggesting water and calm. Orange, yellow, and lime green colored panels bring light and vibrant hues to the room. Mirrored panels above the vanity and along tub walls reflect and repeat surface patterns, creating new vistas. Birch wood and maple floors, which extend from the master bedroom, link the spaces visually and add the warmth of natural materials.

As the clients requested, Rorrison has created a visually uncluttered space that is both clean and well proportioned, bold and distinctly livable.

ARCHITECT: Buschow Henley
LOCATION: London, England   DESIGN BUDGET: $20,000   SQUARE FEET/METERS: 280/26
PHOTOGRAPHY: Mark Bolton Photography

Previous Spread Medicine chests and storage for toiletries are covered by colorful panels that seem to float above the expanse of blue mosaic tiles. To bring different-sized windows into visual conformity, Rorrison reconfigured the reveal of the smaller window, enlarging and angling it to match the other opening.

Above A ceramic semi-encased sink provides visual inversion from a predominance of angles, as does the pattern of ventilation holes along the birch panels.

Right Brightly colored panels bring light and vibrance to the room.

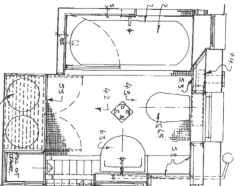

IN GRAND STYLE

Old-World opulence and 20th-century needs can blend quite beautifully, as designer Nicholas Walker proves in this Pasadena Showcase House. "The room was designed as a luxurious retreat for the parents of two active children," says Walker, "and relates to the overall grand European style of the home."

Walker has kept the suite's generous size from becoming cavernous by creating an inviting series of smaller, harmonizing spaces. An octagonal vanity area, rescued from an unused turret, serves as the suite's elegant foyer. Its dome rises 15 feet above the floor, and is finished in gold leaf to add luxurious shimmer to the room's natural light. The floor is of imported French limestone, with a jade granite inlay design and border. A separate shower adjoins the whirlpool area, as does a private water closet containing both toilet and bidet.

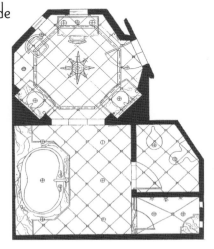

Throughout the suite, Walker has eschewed faux finishes in favor of the natural elegance of stone. Says Walker, "We wanted to use the finest elements in keeping with the home's classic decor."

ARCHITECT/INTERIOR DESIGNER: Nicholas Walker & Associates
LOCATION: Pasadena, California   DESIGN BUDGET: not disclosed   SQUARE FEET/METERS: 450/42
PHOTOGRAPHY: Michael E. Garland

In this view from the foyer, granite counters and tub surrounds unify the spaces. The faucets are 18-karat gold plate with rose quartz handles.

The top and sides of the double vanity cabinet are faced in tile, creating a "dresser" that gives storage drawers below a built-in appearance. An angular cornice, reflected in the mirror, sits atop the shower and water closet niches.

COLORS OF THE COAST

Although it is in an urban setting, this bathroom "brings in an array of bright, exciting colors, imitating the look of an Italian beach cabin," says architect and designer Elisa Morchio. Used by a family of five adults, the room's configuration——with doors placed at opposite ends——allows it to function comfortably for several people at one time.

The bath's long, narrow shape required some architectural restructuring for convenience. Along one wall, Morchio created a series of separate niches to accommodate the tub, a separate shower, and a semi-private water closet. Because of the room's ground-floor location, windows were designed with a clever grid pattern of solid and glass bricks, providing both light and privacy.

Pale, sand-colored tiles dominate the room's color scheme. A dark grout emphasizes the rectangular shape of the tiles. A series of contrasting tile stripes in pale pink, blue and yellow add visual interest. The tile pattern appears again on the double vanity, where the seashore colors are repeated on alternate drawers. In addition to the bath's playful style, its simple surfaces are easy to maintain, making it a practical execution of an original design.

ARCHITECT/INTERIOR DESIGNER: Galleria "Sul Po"
LOCATION: Turin, Italy   DESIGN BUDGET: $8,300   SQUARE FEET/METERS: 161/15
PHOTOGRAPHY: Manuela Cerri

35

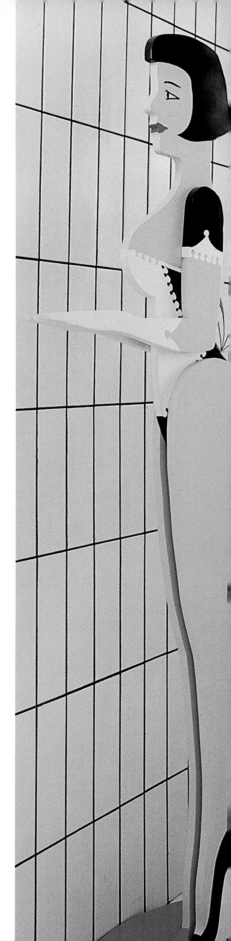

Left Niches, open to the ceiling, divide functions without obstructing light. At the far end, a storage wall, with its full-width mirror and pale ivory doors, recedes into the overall design. Reflected in the mirror, a faux shutter in the water closet adds another series of horizontal elements to the room's predominant verticals.

Below A contemporary Venetian wall sconce adds a jewel-toned geometry to the space's linear theme.

Right The tub surround repeats the room's vertical pattern. The grid of the brick-and-glass window adds a medley of horizontals. A "maid," designed by Morchio, holds towels for bathers.

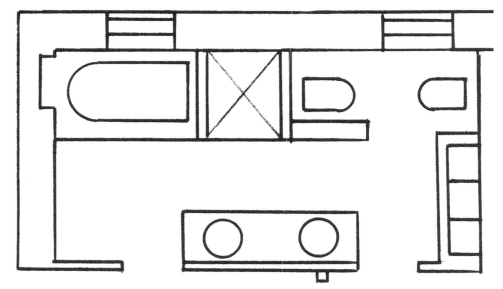

THE BROADER VIEW

he picture window is the key element in this master bath, explain interior designers Marilyn and Stephanie Wolf. "The clients, a couple with two children, wanted a calming, peaceful space that would relate to the environment," says Stephanie Wolf. To accommodate them, the designers conscripted an adjacent, unused bedroom into the existing tiny master bath to create a spacious haven with a view of the countryside.

A neutral color palette was chosen so that the view could speak for itself. Marble, the room's dominant material, introduces warm tones into the space; marble countertops have radius edges. Laminate-faced cabinets and a simple textured wallcovering provide easy to maintain surfaces.

Panels of unadorned mirrors over the vanity and by the tub seemingly double the room's size and call attention to the ever-changing pastoral scene. Overhead, a skylight, set into an angled recess, casts additional light into the room's interior. To enhance the room's luxuriousness, the designers included some special touches, such as a stereo system and heated floors.

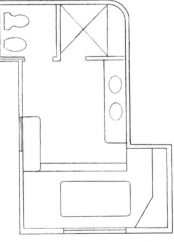

INTERIOR DESIGNER: Interiors by M & S, Inc.
LOCATION: Muttontown, New York   DESIGN BUDGET: $30,000   SQUARE FEET/METERS: 225/21
PHOTOGRAPHY: Phillip Ennis

As they relax in the whirlpool tub, bathers can enjoy the sky above and the earth below. For privacy, an unobtrusive shade lowers to conceal the eight-foot window. Tubside mirrored panels hide the medicine chest and storage, and offer a different perspective of the countryside. Marble on the floor, tub surround, and counters is carefully arranged so that striations lead the eye toward the view.

AN OBJECT "POSATO"

This cylindrical bath is "composed in a tranquil state, or 'posato,'" says architect and designer Angelo Tartaglia, who has created a room within a room so particularly placed and structured that no one realizes from the outside what is inside——a functional bathroom. "I wanted to create a circular bath without renouncing the architecture that makes good design," Tartaglia says. "The more difficult the shape, the harder you try to ensure its functionality."

Constructed within a small loft for the family's adult son, the bathroom's structure separates private functions without subdividing the suite. Technically, the room was a challenge: suspended on an iron frame above the floor and below the ceiling, its form excludes the use of large, heavy materials. Aesthetically, it conforms to the home's contemporary style and spare elegance. With the exception of one marble shelf above the vanity backsplash for accessories, the room's ornamentation is the design itself.

ARCHITECT/INTERIOR DESIGNER: Angelo Tartaglia
LOCATION: Campobasso, Italy   DESIGN BUDGET: $16,000   SQUARE FEET/METERS: 52/5
PHOTOGRAPHY: Edoardo D'Antona

The room's solitary window opens like a porthole. A smooth pane of frosted glass provides privacy. Centered on the rear wall, a vertical row of glass blocks ornaments the surface. Glass blocks along the ceiling's perimeter accentuate the room's shape and allow an interchange of light between the bath and the surrounding living area. From the entry, the vanity has the aspect of a sleek, built-in buffet, its handles serving as towel racks. A wedge-shaped shower stall bisects the circle, its clear glass door keeping the shower's shape open to view.

COLLECTOR'S SHOWCASE

This opulent master bathroom
created by designer Nicholas Walker for the CALM Design Showcase

House 1996 elegantly expresses its designer's sensitivity to his clients'

needs. Since the professional couple are avid collectors, their entire home

is a gallery for their carefully gathered treasures.

The master bath and an adjoining sitting room relate to the house's

Mediterranean architecture, says Walker. Together, the rooms allow for a calm, comfortable transition

from public areas to private spaces. A color palette of khaki and beige was selected to create a soothing

atmosphere and a suitable background for the array of artwork. Pewter fixtures softly contrast with the

gleam of the French limestone and Italian marble. To introduce tones and textures from the sitting area,

Walker placed several upholstered pieces and an antique rug to the bath. A reproduction chinoiserie table

anchors the small sitting space, which is oriented toward the view through the room's French doors.

Overall, says Walker, "The suite is designed to convey the feeling of an Old World classic."

ARCHITECT/INTERIOR DESIGNER: Nicholas Walker & Associates
LOCATION: Montecito, California   DESIGN BUDGET: not disclosed   SQUARE FEET/METERS: 400/37
PHOTOGRAPHY: Michael E. Garland

Previous Spread Objets d'art from the owners' collection are at home amid the room's opulence. A central sitting area is defined by an antique Persian rug and a Baccarat chandelier. Wall sconces provide soft lighting by the custom-designed cabinets and antique reproduction mirrors framing the French doors.

Right The mosaic patterns on the tub surround and in the shower are reminiscent of the home's Mediterranean style. Details of the design are repeated in the marble wainscoting.

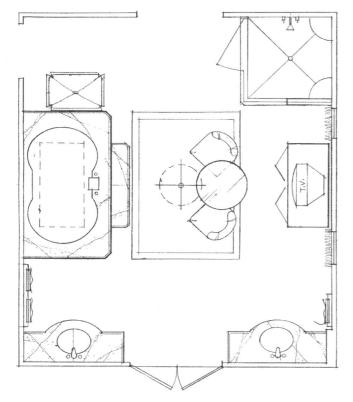

BACHELOR'S QUARTERS

In this '50s ranch home, interior designer Jackie Naylor has turned a spare bedroom into an elegant bachelor's retreat with a European flair. "I like to play dynamic opposites against one another," Naylor says, "taking two elements you might not expect and making them work together." Here, Mediterranean touches such as the stone shower floor juxtapose with contemporary glass blocks. A traditional cherrywood cabinet holds two modern semi-encaste sinks. Above each, a traditional recessed medicine chest is flanked by contemporary incandescent tube lighting. Limestone tiles cover the floor and walls, a classically simple pattern of slate forming an eye-level border.

Because the bathroom adjoins a deck and pool, Naylor has kept surfaces smooth for ease of maintenance. The palette, a neutral spectrum of earth tones, provides for a natural transition between indoor and outdoor spaces. The glass-block shower wall forms an entry hall from the master bedroom, and also lets sunlight from the deckside French doors filter into the hall. Overhead, the ceiling follows the roofline, adding another unexpected dimension to Naylor's vision.

INTERIOR DESIGNER: Jackie Naylor Interiors Inc.
LOCATION: Atlanta, Georgia   DESIGN BUDGET: $75,000   SQUARE FEET/METERS: 192/18
PHOTOGRAPHY: © Robert Thien

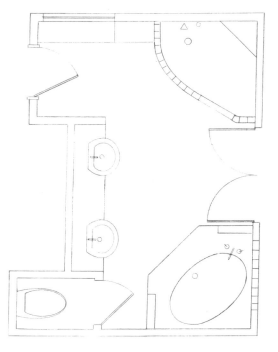

Previous Spread The bath's elegant use of angles and curves is apparent in this view from the whirlpool tub. A soffit and side walls encase the vanity, framing it and creating a shelf for artwork. Between the shower and tub, French doors open onto a poolside deck and hot tub.

Above Tiled in a random pattern of broken stones, the shower floor takes on the look of a Mediterranean patio. Because of the shower's generous size, a door wasn't necessary, permitting an unobstructed view of the wall detail.

Right Glass-block windows flood the room with natural sunlight while affording privacy. Set in a diagonal pattern that is repeated on opposite walls, limestone tiles form the tub surround. The water closet is housed at the far end of the vanity, which is an ergonomically comfortable 36" high.

CONTEMPORARY APPEAL

"*inearity and deceptive simplicity make this bathroom's* atmosphere very sophisticated," says architect and designer Angelo Tartaglia of his sleekly styled master bath for the husband of the family. Tartaglia never sacrifices function to aesthetics. Yet the aesthetic appeal is of primary importance, as demonstrated by this design.

The bath is a room of dominant horizontals. The floor and walls appear as one, in a multi-leveled "L"-shaped space whose gray and white palette is animated by the marble's striations. Monolithic pieces of marble keep lines contemporary and pure, making a stunning backdrop for the room's elegant fixtures.

To give the bath the appearance of a room within a room, Tartaglia has mirror paneled the primary adjacent walls above wainscoting and shelves. A marble bench on the long wall conceals storage at one end and supports the toilet and bidet at the other. As requested, the room has a shower only and, most luxurious of all, a heated floor.

ARCHITECT/INTERIOR DESIGNER: Angelo Tartaglia
LOCATION: Campobasso, Italy   DESIGN BUDGET: $27,000   SQUARE FEET/METERS: 85/8
PHOTOGRAPHY: Edoardo D'Antona

The soft, matte black finish of the panel below the sink is repeated in the toe-kick, window frame, and accessories. Uniquely styled halogen lights are reverse images of the panel, giving the room one of its few curvilinear elements.

A head-on view from the entrance reveals the bathroom's assortment of planes. Shelves and niches in the shower and by the tub provide areas for storage and display.

THE NATURAL ASPECT

To create a secluded bath in the heart of the city, architect and homeowner René Fernandes Filho opened his bedroom suite onto a lush courtyard, making the sun and greenery part of his private world. "Its functionality and luminosity make this space very special to me," says Filho.

Because he lives in a mild climate, Filho brought interior and exterior spaces together in such a way that, while they can be closed to one another, allows them to interact. There is no separation between bedroom and bath. The vanity counter, in full view of the bedroom, overlooks the courtyard. The water closet is tucked discreetly along the opposite wall. At the counter's far end, a doorway opens to the shower, which in turn leads, through sliding doors, to a deck with an ofuro (a Japanese bathing tub).

Filho has dramatically accentuated the courtyard's plant life by choosing a deep, rich adobe shade for courtyard walls and creating a colorful patchwork of red, orange, and white tiles on the shower wall to combine elements of both spaces. "Altogether, it is a colorful and merry atmosphere," says Filho.

ARCHITECT: René Fernandes Filho
LOCATION: São Paulo, Brazil   DESIGN BUDGET: $40,200   SQUARE FEET/METERS: 721/67
PHOTOGRAPHY: Alain Brugier

Previous Spread Access to the courtyard, shower, and Japanese tub is at either end of the vanity. Because the spaces are open to one another, rubber floor tiles were selected for ease of maintenance.

Right Returning the room to its basic elements, the sink sits exposed and unadorned in a white marble counter. Instead of a cabinet, tables on casters provide storage. Through the window, the colorful patchwork of tiles is visible.

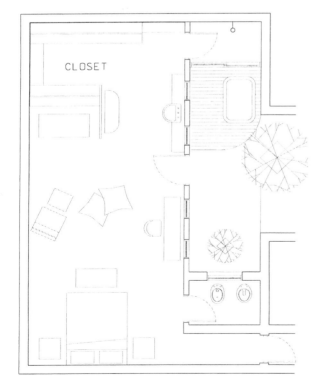

CLOSET

AN OPEN ARRANGEMENT

small master bath can still have a big design impact if homeowners are willing to be open to new ideas," says designer Lynn Wallace. In this compact room, Wallace successfully illustrates her point, compensating for lack of space with thoughtful planning, and creating a haven for the busy couple. "My clients wanted a rich, Mediterranean look," she says, which was achieved by using abundant marble. The bathroom doorway was widened to create a sense of entry and outfitted with pocket doors for privacy. A monochromatic color scheme visually expands the area. The textures of marble and hand-painted wooden cabinetry add variety and depth. Ceramic floors, too, have been finished to resemble marble. In one corner, a double vanity angles along the walls. A counter-level storage column, located in the center of the vanity, holds a television and additional space for toiletries.

A three-paneled glass shower shield glimmers in the sunlight refracted through glass blocks. Custom-finished, oil-rubbed bronze fixtures complement the room's tones.

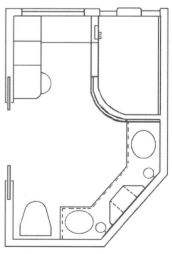

INTERIOR DESIGNER: Kitchens & Baths by Lynn
LOCATION: Thousand Palms, California   DESIGN BUDGET: $35,000   SQUARE FEET/METERS: 135/13
PHOTOGRAPHY: Chris Covey

A shower-and-whirlpool-tub unit was created in the room's limited space to serve both functions. The tub's curved corner is repeated in the step leading into it; marble tiles extending from the walls to the tub's floor further integrate the fixture into the room's overall design. A single panel of glass blocks filters natural light into the space, reflecting it off the beveled-glass, three-panel shower screen. Behind the door to the tub's left is an area for linen storage.

IN THE PINK

rawing upon the '50s for his inspiration, architect and designer Angelo Tartaglia created a pink-and-black gem of a bathroom with thoroughly modern efficiency. "This bathroom is used every day, so there is a lot of storage space," Tartaglia says. "But the way we designed it, there seems to be none."

Tartaglia took advantage of the bathroom's view, opening it to a balcony that expands the space literally and visually. On each side of the vanity, columns that appear to be simple structural elements in fact conceal storage spaces. Close inspection also reveals storage beneath the vanity, whose oval shape is a pleasant counterpoint to the room's predominant linearity. Gleaming pink porcelain tiles cover the floors and line the walls. Tartaglia has chosen to use tiles of the same dimensions for both the walls and the floor, keeping visual distractions to a minimum.

Because Tartaglia prefers to separate the water closet from view, he has created an innovative wall of sliding doors that are framed in black aluminum. In combination with the ventilator panel across the top of the space, the wall becomes a strong design element of its own.

ARCHITECT/INTERIOR DESIGNER: Angelo Tartaglia
LOCATION: Campobasso, Italy   DESIGN BUDGET: $17,000   SQUARE FEET/METERS: 79/7
PHOTOGRAPHY: Edoardo D'Antona

Previous Spread & Above Mirror placement above and below the vanity makes the oval surface appear to float between two storage towers. The unique window design on the balcony wall adds a distinctive architectural element to the room.

Opposite A series of glass panels includes two hammered glass sliding doors that provide necessary privacy along the shower/water closet wall. The area is set one step above the floor.

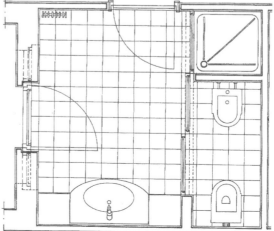

A GLASS HOUSE

"Aesthetics and function are inseparable in all our designs," says designer Barry Brukoff, whose philosophy is immediately apparent in this master bath created for a professional couple. The bath, which also serves as a powder room for guests, is an elegant private retreat, aesthetically in synch with its northern California setting.

To expand the compact room visually and to admit light with minimal sacrifice to privacy, Brukoff and architect Ron Kappe fashioned a curved glass-block wall, the room's focal point. A frameless shower stall, a necessary utility, allows the line of the wall to remain unbroken.

Balancing the colorlessness of the glass block are the deep, warm tones of the fixtures and slate tiles. Their colors are repeated in the eaves seen indistinctly through the glass. The slate's rough texture and slightly uneven edges contrast with other smooth surfaces. Cherry cabinets add another element of warmth. The gray tones of the cast concrete counter with its integral bowl are picked up in a row of slate tiles on the toe kick, backsplash, and tub surround.

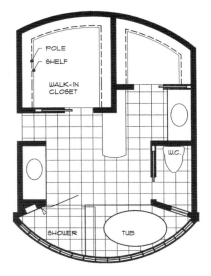

ARCHITECT: Russel-Kappe Design Group   INTERIOR DESIGNER: Brukoff Design Associates, Inc.
LOCATION: Berkeley, California   DESIGN BUDGET: not disclosed   SQUARE FEET/METERS: 180/17
PHOTOGRAPHY: Barry Brukoff

Carefully integrated into the design, a frameless glass shower stall is not immediately apparent, allowing an unbroken view of the curved glass wall. Slate floors extend to the tub surround and backsplash.

Old and new live together comfortably

in this urban apartment created by designer Leonard Braunschweiger. The owner, a retired international banker, travels frequently, using the apartment for evening entertaining and accommodating visitors. The small guest bath is now an integral part of his home office, which converts to sleeping quarters.

"We needed to create a space that was minimal but rich, with natural woods and stone that would complement the apartment's existing style as well as the owner's collection of objets d'art," Braunschweiger says. Adhering to a color scheme of muted, deep tones, he gave the room an appropriately antique look, by covering the wall and floors with Italian tiles that, with their rough edges and surfaces, resemble stone. Lighting, too, is subtle, the sconces in scale with the room's compact size.

The view from the guest room into the bath is symmetrical and in harmony with its surroundings. To keep the aspect open and clean, Braunschweiger crafted a pivot-hinged bathroom door which, when opened, fits into a shallow, mirrored recess to become flush with the wall.

INTERIOR DESIGNER: Leonard Braunschweiger + Company Inc.
LOCATION: New York, New York   DESIGN BUDGET: $30,000   SQUARE FEET/METERS: 45/4
PHOTOGRAPHY: © Ashod Kassabian Photo/Video

Previous Spread Blending with the warm tones of the cherrywood panel below the sink, an antique Oriental shop sign is the room's one ornament. The towel bar is conveniently suspended in front of the fossil-stone vanity. Because the bath is visible from the guest room, Braunschweiger carefully framed the vanity in the doorway, keeping lines simple and colors in harmony with those of the home office and guest room.

Right Instead of mirroring the entire shower wall, Braunschweiger used an eight-foot-high mirrored panel to create the effect of an entry into another room. Clear shower doors remove visual obstructions.

BEDROOM

STUDY

COLLECTORS' CORNER

"Powder rooms can be the perfect canvases for expressing an owner's personality," says designer Karin Ramsey, referring to this tiny bath in a renovated historic home. "Since this one is particularly diminutive and in use only for a brief time, it can be over-designed without being overwhelming."

It's a room to satisfy the collector-souls of the owners, an empty-nester couple. It also surprises and entertains guests. Because the space extends from the kitchen, Ramsey has adapted furnishings to satisfy function and blended a diverse array of elements, from antique to futuristic. Matte ceramic floor tiles continue into the space from the kitchen. New walls have been finished to blend with old plaster.

Rather than trying to disguise the room's petite size with a wall of mirrors, Ramsey has turned the minimal space into an asset, hanging groupings of decorative mirrors that become a utilitarian part of the eclectic display. Other found objects blend with the room's neutral tones and playful character, earning their rightful niche.

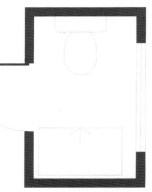

INTERIOR DESIGNER: Karin Ramsey Interiors

80   LOCATION: Greensboro, North Carolina   DESIGN BUDGET: $2,000   SQUARE FEET/METERS: 24/2

PHOTOGRAPHY: Bob Sterenberg

An 1860s washstand is modernized with fixtures finished to replicate the look of antique pewter. Plaster medallions adorn the faux-finished chair rail.

SOFTENING THE EDGES

"The integration of curved and rectilinear planes in this dual master bathroom underlies the need for a sense of soft structure," explain interior designers Lee Bierly and Chris Drake about this suite designed for a professional couple. With architect John MacDonald, the designers created spacious, his-and-hers master baths, united by a dual-entry shower.

The rooms' interplay of hard lines and soft edges is apparent in the choices made throughout. Marble is juxtaposed with glass, wood with nickel; reflective surfaces contrast with adjacent matte finishes. Restful pale-green and beige tones invite relaxation. A gentle combination of downlights and backlighting softens the rooms' impact. Throughout, generous floor space, countertops, and storage areas meet the couple's individual needs.

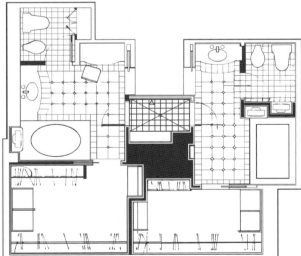

The ultimate indulgence is also somewhat whimsical: a heat-sensitive mirror by each bathtub hides a television set, which is only visible when the t.v. is in use.

ARCHITECT: Moorehouse MacDonald Architects   INTERIOR DESIGNER: Bierly-Drake Associates
LOCATION: Eastern Massachusetts   DESIGN BUDGET: not disclosed   SQUARE FEET/METERS: 2,500/232
PHOTOGRAPHY: Sam Gray

Over his vanity, two magnifying mirrors pivot from a central point; a nickel-plated frame repeats the shapes of lights, handles, and mirrors. The pocket door, with its panes of translucent glass, echoes the pattern of the opposite etched glass door. In her suite, a curved towel bar follows the curve of the vanity, placing towels within easy reach. To further define the separate spaces, a lighter tone of marble was chosen for her countertops and for the border on the floor. In both areas, doors obscure the water closets.

A TRANSPARENT PLAN

restrained palette and an unrestrained sense of space were the qualities that architect Hugh Broughton sought in the redesign of this tiny basement apartment. The space had only two windows——one in the living room, the other in the bedroom. To resolve the problem, says Broughton, "We relied on artificial light and a plan which opened up the flat to create fluid and transparent connections between rooms."

Once an unappealing warren of rooms along a dark interior hallway, the kitchen and bath now connect as a seemingly unified light-filled space. Broughton chose to emphasize the corridor's linearity with clear glass doors and screens between the spaces and a single line of recessed downlights stretching the length of the rooms.

The pale gray striations of the Carrara marble on the vanity and tub surround relieve the whiteness of ceramic tiles and fixtures. Broughton introduced a few cobalt-blue accents, notably in the storage cabinet.

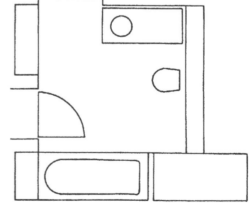

ARCHITECT: Hugh Broughton Architects
LOCATION: London, England   DESIGN BUDGET: $13,845   SQUARE FEET/METERS: 90/8
PHOTOGRAPHY: Carlos Dominguez

A fixed glass panel between the bathroom and kitchen allows ambient light to pass between the two windowless spaces; the blind closes for privacy.

SENSUOUS CURVES

master bath that was "warm sensuous, and luxurious" was the request of the owners, the parents of young children. Interior designer Gabriella Toro responded with a graceful design of light and curves, "an atmosphere in which masculine and feminine elements complement one another," says Toro.

Although the curves' appeal is decidedly aesthetic, their initial use was dictated by space constrictions: curved lines allowed Toro to maximize limited floor and countertop space. The curved tub surround is generous without protruding into the room. The cabinets also follow the curve of the countertop, working with the mirrors to become sculptural elements. "They go beyond necessary bathroom fixtures to become an integral part of the concave and convex surfaces," says Toro.

"A very light hand in the detailing," and a series of straight-line elements that include wooden beams, window frames, and display shelves work together to balance the undulating lines. A skylight provides an interplay of light and shadows.

INTERIOR DESIGNER: Cippananda Interior Design
LOCATION: Santa Monica, California   DESIGN BUDGET: $50,000   SQUARE FEET/METERS: 158/15
PHOTOGRAPHY: Derek Rath

Previous Spread Although granite surfaces dominate, their impact is softened by the warmth of mahogany cabinets, exposed beams, abundant natural light, and a skylight view of trees and clouds. A storage niche is located beneath the deck of the extra-deep tub for convenient access to towels and toiletries.

Left An exterior window ornaments the shower stall. Overhead, ceiling beams extend into the space. The shower's frameless double doors meet in the middle at an angle.

Right Cabinets and mirrors extend to countertop level, eliminating the need for backsplashes. The cabinets also help to define areas of use along the marble counter.

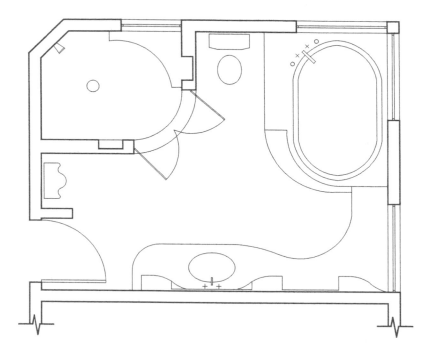

A MODERN CLASSIC

"Along with an abundance of light and air, my clients wanted a master bath with elements of both modern and classic design," says architect and designer Léo Shehtman. To meet the couple's basic design criteria, Shehtman has created a setting with timeless appeal by using a dramatically simple color scheme of black and white. To enhance the room's qualities of light and air, he has limited the number of materials used. Spaces are uncluttered, and open to a soaring expanse of windows that frame a planter box.

The essential material of choice is marble, used in the classic floor design and, sparingly, on counters and sills. The room takes its style from the dominant window. The strong, rectangular elements are repeated in the small window by the tub and in the design created by the mirrored-and-matte-black cabinetry. In lower panels, frosted glass eliminates the need for a window treatment. Overhead, classically styled crown molding softens the ceiling's angularity, while recessed lighting supplements the room's natural illumination.

"By subtly blending these elements of modern and classic," says Shehtman, "we achieved a design that is truly innovative and aesthetically pleasing."

ARCHITECT/INTERIOR DESIGNER: Léo Shehtman Arquitetura & Design
LOCATION: São Paulo, Brazil   DESIGN BUDGET: $42,000   SQUARE FEET/METERS: 161/15
PHOTOGRAPHY: João Ribeiro

Previous Spread Marble floors in a black-and-white pattern establish the room's classic look. Mirrored vanity doors, an Art Deco-style wall sconce, and a small angled window alcove add modern touches.

Left Here, the full impact of the greenhouse wall on the room is obvious. The generous use of mirrors doubles the impact of the natural sunlight and lush greenery. Against the black cabinetry, mirrored vanity doors below the counter seem to vanish.

Right The marble backsplash extends to frame the full-width mirror. Thoughtful details include contrasting marble handles on fixtures.

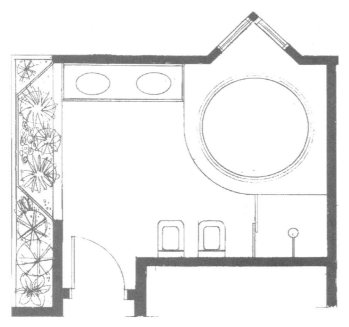

arved from a small space left over from a remodeling

project, this guest-room bath by designers Arthur de Mattos Casas and Agnes Bourne took its peaceful

green theme from the adjoining green-and-white bedroom.

The specific need, says Bourne, "was for a relaxed environment, a place for guests to read while soaking

in the tub." To create that atmosphere in such a compact area, de Mattos Casas says that they relied on

the judicious use of few elements and fewer colors.

The designers opted to blanket the room, including the side of the deep Grecian bath, with green glass

tiles in order to unify the space and to add sparkle to the surfaces. Fixtures and hardware were custom-

designed to fit into the small space. A tall mirrored medicine chest seems to

extend the room vertically. Stainless-steel surfaces reflect light and color while

a frosted-glass window provides privacy.

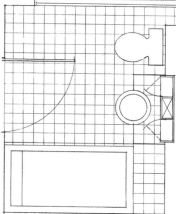

The final effect: a restful retreat whose limited space has not limited its

"spirit of freedom," says Bourne.

ARCHITECT: Cornelia Griffin   INTERIOR DESIGNERS: Studio Arthur de Mattos Casas ◆ Agnes Bourne, Inc.
LOCATION: San Francisco, California   DESIGN BUDGET: $30,000   SQUARE FEET/METERS: 36/3
PHOTOGRAPHY: David Livingston

A brushed stainless-steel bowl sits atop a sandblasted-glass counter set into a cantilevered stainless frame. The vanity's delicate appearance belies its ease of maintenance. The subtle variations and delicate sheen of the hand-cut, hand-poured glass mosaic tiles, which are set into green grout, give the wall the hypnotic appeal of ocean waves.

COUNTRY CHARM

n an English country cottage, designer Johnny Grey has created a "quietly modern" bathroom for a young couple and their two children. "We attempted to ensure that the surfaces should appear soft to offset the 'hard' look of such waterproof materials as glass, marble, stainless steel, and porcelain," says Grey about the room that serves as the family's primary bath.

Gentle curves and a palette of pale, warm tones are the elements Grey introduced to soften the room's look. The delicate pink hues of the Portuguese limestone floors belie the material's imperviousness to wear and water. Along the tub's edge, a roll of pink marble accentuates the color of the floor and ceramic shower tiles. To bring the view inside, Grey widened and lowered the lone window.

Still, durability and function have not been sacrificed for design. The faucet has been located along the center rear of the tub, making it "a sociable, double-ended bath, perfect for bathing two children at once," says Grey. The tub surround was also designed with "plenty of putting-down space." By recessing the sloping shower floor just below floor level, Grey eliminated the need for a shower door, keeping the space visually uncluttered and contributing to its ease of maintenance.

INTERIOR DESIGNER: Johnny Grey & Co.
LOCATION: Southern England   DESIGN BUDGET: $30,000   SQUARE FEET/METERS: 100/9
PHOTOGRAPHY: James Mortimer

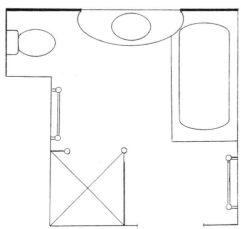

Previous Spread Contrasting elements of stainless steel blend with the room's sleek surfaces. To keep the view as unobstructed as possible, the basin's faucet is positioned off-center against a small marble backsplash.

Above Positioned in front of the widened window, a custom-designed oval-shaped stainless steel basin overlooks a view of the country garden.

Opposite Shades of the pink marble roll along the tub edge appear in the floor and wall tiles, as well as on the wooden medicine cabinet. A heated towel rack warms linens and robes. The work of artist David Hockney inspired the shower screen's acid-etched pattern of waves, the shapes of which are repeated in the lines of the marble tub.

SIMPLY LUMINOUS

Caroline Sidnam, William Petrone and Eric Gartner of Sidnam Petrone Architects have gently lighted this second-floor master bathroom with natural illumination by creating a two-story light well that rises from this interior space to the rooftop skylight above the third floor.

The room's serenity and artful efficiency reflect the Japanese heritage of the couple for whom it was built. To ensure harmony with its surroundings, the bath's maple cabinetry and doors match the house's existing palette of wood. Multi-hued Indian slate on the floor and walls provides a dramatic backdrop for both the pale wood and for the man-made stone in the tub and shower. Mirrors, medicine cabinets, and shelves are frameless and built into walls. Accessories and lights are recessed, smooth and functional.

To make the compact space feel larger, designers kept fixtures simple and free-standing. Adjacent sinks appear to float above the custom cabinet, which hovers above the floor. The toilet base is slightly above floor level as well. Says Petrone, "These choices were deliberate efforts to make the bathroom seem bigger, lighter, and less cluttered."

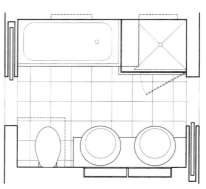

ARCHITECT: Sidnam Petrone Architects
LOCATION: New York, New York   DESIGN BUDGET: not disclosed   SQUARE FEET/METERS: 62/6
PHOTOGRAPHY: Andrew Garn

Custom storage areas are flush with the walls. Pocket doors at either end of the room keep lines simple and unencumbered. By interlocking the shower and tub, the designers have made the space feel larger and, in the process, added an eye-catching visual element. The bathroom draws natural light from a newly built two-story-high light shaft, as well as from the master bedroom and sitting room that surround it.

PACIFIC VILLA

This soft hued guest bath, created for the house of an active family by designers Grover Dear and Agnes Bourne, opts for a profusion of elegant lines and materials over a medley of colors.

"The home's overall architecture dictated the bathroom's style and fixtures," say Dear and Bourne, "while the guest room's fireplace suggested the choice of marble."

The designers have artfully kept the guest bath's opulence in check. The interior design blends into the home's sumptuous nature. A coffered ceiling, milled marble moldings and generous marble pedestal vanity reiterate the many traditional architectural elements in the house. A soft monochromatic palette, coupled with such touches as recessed cove lighting and sconces shaded in linen, allows the room to blend into the adjoining guest suite and to harmonize with the park view outside. Mirror placement and clear glass shower doors further enhance the surroundings while serving their necessary functions. A marble-patterned paper, whose washable practicality belies its appearance, quietly unifies the space.

ARCHITECT: Cornelia Griffin   INTERIOR DESIGNERS: Archasia Hong Kong Limited ◆ Agnes Bourne, Inc.
LOCATION: San Francisco, California   DESIGN BUDGET: $55,000   SQUARE FEET/METERS: 66/6
PHOTOGRAPHY: David Livingston

Previous Spread Inspiration for the bathroom's design came from marble details in the adjoining guest room. The bathroom's artwork conceals the medicine cabinet.

Opposite A mirror on the shower wall reflects the magnificent park view visible from the window opposite. The graceful lines of the vanity and mirror are repeated along the top edge of the shower shield.

The golden tones of artwork, wall sconces, fixtures, and accessories bring warmth to the room's sleek simplicity. A private steam shower and a private water closet with toilet and bidet flank the whirlpool's niche.

REFLECTING THE VIEW

small master bathroom can still have a big impact as does this elegant bath in the urban apartment of a single professional man. "The overall '20s character of the building influenced the basic design," says interior designer Orlando Diaz-Azcuy, "but we used the traditional maple and Calcutta marble in a contemporary manner."

Diaz-Azcuy has designed an artful arrangement of mirrors, creating an intriguing panorama of sight-lines and illusions and giving the traditionally appointed room and materials a distinctly modern touch. Mirrors can be surprising and unobtrusive, such as the panels surrounding the vanity, or bold and direct, as in the mirrored wall of the shower. The most imaginative, however, is his design of the mirror above the vanity, which actually functions as a pocket door, sliding aside to admit natural light and the view.

Complementing the room's aesthetic appeal is its straightforward practicality. Doorways at both ends allow access from the master bedroom or from the library. Large linen closets flank the vanity. Heated floors warm up bare feet. "It is a luxurious space," explains Diaz-Azcuy, "elegant, open, and rich in materials."

INTERIOR DESIGNER: Orlando Diaz-Azcuy Design, Inc.
LOCATION: Northern California   DESIGN BUDGET: $22,500   SQUARE FEET/METERS: 150/14
PHOTOGRAPHY: © John Sutton 1998

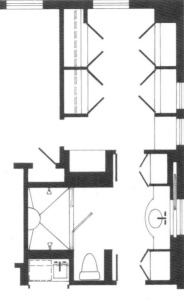

Previous Spread Maple cabinetry extends into the master dressing room, creating continuity between the spaces. The vanity's simple curve matches that of the shower seat on the opposite wall.

Above Mirrors above the vanity and on the opposite shower wall reflect one another, giving the illusion of a corridor of rooms. Beneath the vanity, mirrored doors and marble baseboards make the cabinet seem to float above the floor.

Right The shower's generous size compensates for the absence of a tub. The mirrored shower wall reflects the vanity, which has a recessed mirror that captures the light and the view.

A FRESH ANGLE

enlarging this master bathroom without expanding

its dimensions was the challenge for designers Roland and Joan DesCombes. Through the inspired place-

ment of the new whirlpool tub and clever use of angles and mirrors, says Joan DesCombes, "We expanded

the space visually, giving the young parents a peaceful, luxurious retreat that seems larger than it is."

The focal point and key architectural element in the updated bathroom is the custom-designed maple

arch above the whirlpool tub. Mimicking another window, the arch extends to the ceiling; beveled mirrors

inset into each pane reflect various perspectives of the space. By angling the tub into the room's center,

the designers also created ample room behind the new wall

to incorporate a linen closet and a spacious walk-in shower.

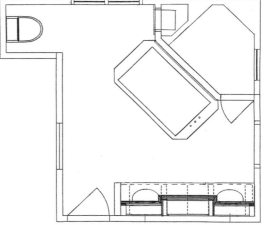

Pewter hardware and honey-maple cabinetry and trim match

the color and style of the bedroom furnishings, lending conti-

nuity to the entire master suite. Warm-toned granite and marble

underscore the room's elegant materials and clean lines.

ARCHITECT/INTERIOR DESIGNER: Architectural Artworks Incorporated
LOCATION: Central Florida   DESIGN BUDGET: $27,000   SQUARE FEET/METERS: 150/14
PHOTOGRAPHY: © Everett & Soulé, Orlando

A simple display shelf divides the vanity into his-and-hers alcoves, its arch repeating the lines of the reflected arch over the tub. Giallo Veneziano granite counters and Travertine marble floors blend with honey-maple woodwork, which has been finished with lime paste to highlight the wood grain. Pilasters flanking the vanity's center drawers pull out to reveal his-and-hers shelves for toiletries.

Previous Spread On a simple shelf out of harm's way, the television is visible from both vanity and tub. The generous surround provides ample room for toiletries and accessories.

Above & Right Glass doors separate the shower from the main bath. Geometric shapes are a backdrop for an array of subtle patterns that change with the ebb and flow of natural light while the cityscape remains in view.

Far Right The structure of the stainless steel sinks is showcased below the counter. The lines and finishes are repeated on the backsplash and in the fixtures. Custom glass-and-mirror double doors seem to float from their stainless frames.

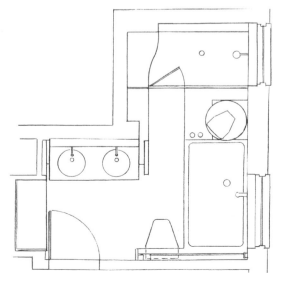

A SENSE OF PLACE

The magnificent Pacific coast and neoclassical elements of late 19th-century architecture inspired designers Armando Ruiz y Perez and Agnes Bourne for this imaginative bathroom.

Artist Jill Beardsky's ocean mural, which covers all four walls, establishes the room's theme. "This is a bathroom that's used by the family and visiting grandchildren," says Bourne. "The intention was to prompt images of 'The Owl and the Pussycat' or 'Three Men in a Tub'."

To make the bath a comfortable retreat for adults as well, the designers chose neoclassically elegant fixtures. An abundance of marble on the floor and wainscoting reiterates the home's Italianate elements. Generous enough for storage, the vanity cabinet is designed to resemble fine furniture, an effect enhanced by the arched dresser mirror above it. The fluorescent lighting has been color-corrected to balance the room's cool hues. "This room tells the story of the house, its location and its era." says Bourne.

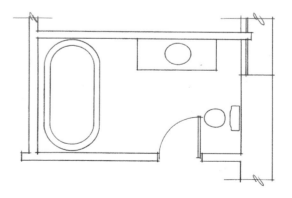

ARCHITECT: Cornelia Griffin   INTERIOR DESIGNERS: Armando Ruiz Diseno, S.A. • Agnes Bourne, Inc.
LOCATION: San Francisco, California   DESIGN BUDGET: $30,000   SQUARE FEET/METERS: 88/8
PHOTOGRAPHY: David Livingston

The free-standing cast-iron tub reminds the owner of the "Rub-a-dub-dub, three men in a tub" nursery rhyme—big enough to bathe several grandchildren, or two adults, at once.

ARCHITECT: Robert C. Wakely Architects   INTERIOR DESIGNER: Riverside Custom Design + Remodeling, Ltd.
LOCATION: Grosse Pointe, Michigan   DESIGN BUDGET: $48,000   SQUARE FEET/METERS: 323/30
PHOTOGRAPHY: Jeff Garland Photography

143

Previous Spread Ample ledges alongside the tub, concealing storage areas below, are integrated into the plan with a pattern of inset tiles that repeats the angles of the vaulted ceiling. From the tub, bathers can listen to music or view the television located in a recess above the doorway.

This Spread Shallow soffits extend below the crown molding detailed to blend with the cabinet molding. Her vanity incorporates a dressing table and abundant storage.

ROMAN HOLIDAY

n this pied-à-terre in the heart of Rome, architect and designer Angelo Tartaglia has created a minimalist and efficient bath for a single professional man. Tartaglia let the space's unusual shape define its design. "I decided that the pieces would fit together in an intelligent way, like the solution to a puzzle."

All fixtures are standard size, black, silver or clear to recede into gray ceramic wall and floor tiles. A small triangular seat rests at one end of the whirlpool. At the other, a glass-block wall curves between the bath and living areas, creating an alcove for shelves and a second source of light. "It was a technical drawback that was turned into an attractive feature," Tartaglia says.

The potential for surface storage exists through a unique system of tiles equipped with bolts, allowing the owner to interchange an assortment of shelves, racks, and bars.

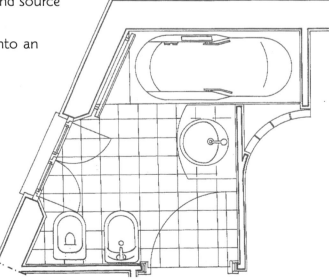

ARCHITECT/INTERIOR DESIGNER: Angelo Tartaglia
LOCATION: Rome, Italy DESIGN BUDGET: $15,000 SQUARE FEET/METERS: 47/4
PHOTOGRAPHY: Edoardo D'Antona

The vanity-width mirror covers the wall from counter to ceiling, making the sink look as though it's suspended between two rooms. The radiator/heated towel bar is reflected in the mirror. The vanity top curves so as not to hinder access to the tub.

EAST MEETS WEST

In this bathroom in a California guest suite, jet-lagged visitors are offered a place of renewal and retreat, explains architect David Hertz. "The scale and function invite references to Japanese guest houses, where a sense of privacy is balanced with community." The self-contained quarters blend with the '50s ranch style of the home.

There are no unnecessary details in Hertz's coherent, minimalist design. In the bathroom, as in the other rooms of the suite, surfaces are seamless and smooth. Colors form a restrained palette of taupes, grays and white that blend with the austerity of stucco and smooth plaster. A warm contrast to the room's serene coolness comes from the sleek custom cabinet of Douglas fir. The glass-paneled door is laminated with rice paper to softly filter the light from adjoining rooms. Strategically placed pinpoint lighting adds to the room's sanctuary-like atmosphere.

"The minimal, natural quality of this bath offers guests a place for solitude and quiet contemplation," Hertz concludes.

ARCHITECT: Syndesis, Inc.
LOCATION: Bel Air, California   DESIGN BUDGET: not disclosed   SQUARE FEET/METERS: 917/85
PHOTOGRAPHY: © Tom Bonner

Previous Spread Vertical-grained Douglas fir and a sleek wall sconce keep the room's lines and textures from becoming too severe. A glass panel at the end of the cabinet separates functions without blocking light or creating a visual distraction.

Right Architect-designed elements of Syndecrete®, a precast lightweight concrete, include a "deep and solid" tub, floor tiles, and a monolithic window that extends downward from a small skylight and clerestory. The copper tubing heats to warm towels when the shower is in use.

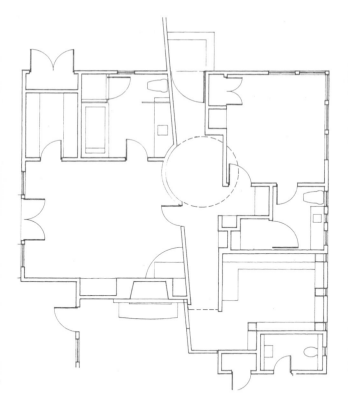

Previous Spread Mirrors extend to the ceiling above both vanities. Panels on either side of the stationary center sections conceal medicine chests and pull out to become three-way mirrors. Linen storage is housed in a generous maple closet that matches the vanity's cabinetry. The doorway to the right leads to the master closet.

Above Pieces from the owners' collection of Latin American art are displayed above a teak storage bench adjacent to the shower.

Right In this view from the tub, the room's generous dimensions are apparent. The far doorway leads to the master bedroom. Shoji screens open to reveal a garden view. All thresholds are made of purplewood.

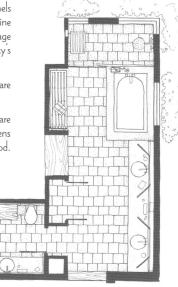

A NATURAL KINSHIP

*N*atural materials give this bathroom a kinship to its surroundings," says architect and homeowner Angela Danadjieva of the powder room in her rustic post-and-beam house. Its size is proportional to the home's compact footprint, its style in harmony with the lush Marin County mountains that surround it.

The bath is a series of open planes. Danadjieva has extended surfaces and textures from the living areas into the bath, preserving the interior's overall visual integrity. Constructed with a doorway height rear wall that resembles a built-in buffet, the bathroom sink can also serve as a wet bar. Rough-sawn pine boards cover the walls. The counter, shower, and cabinets are built of redwood. Surfaces that are exposed to water have been treated with a clear, protective finish.

Glimpses of Bay Area Victorian style emerge in the room's accessories, notably in the use of antique doorknobs. The blend, says Danadjieva, "ensures that the home's historic, traditional themes are not lost."

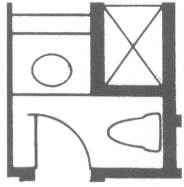

ARCHITECT: Danadjieva & Koenig Associates
LOCATION: Tiburon, California   DESIGN BUDGET: $8,000   SQUARE FEET/METERS: 64/6
PHOTOGRAPHY: J.F. Housel

A simple redwood trough creates an uplighted wall over the sink. The wall behind the sink is doorway-height and open to the stairwell behind it.

Previous Spread A turn-of-the-century copper tub offers an irresistible invitation to soak and enjoy the view. The doorless shower stall, with natural stone walls and floor, assumes the look of a secluded grotto.

Right That the bath embraces the environment is apparent in this view toward the trees. Framed within a single sliding-glass panel, the ledge creates a place for quiet reflection on the wonders of nature.

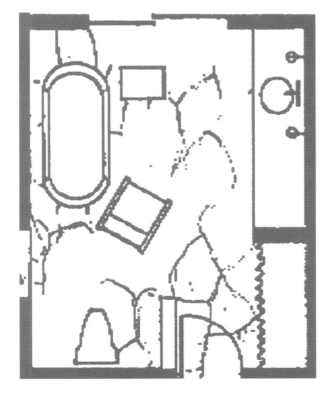

Previous Spread Showcased against the room's whiteness, a framed sketch by artist Carlos Araujo and an original Charles Eames chair stand out. The tub wall and surround are faced with marble.

Right A full view of the dressing room's bath wing shows a range of curvilinear elements in fixtures and accessories. Louvered sliding doors hide the water closet from view; both door panels open for access to the roll-out storage shelves at each end of the vanity.

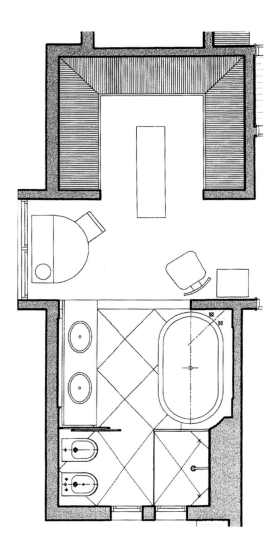

Chris Covey
1780 Vista Del Mar
Ventura, California 93001
Tel: (805) 648-3067
Fax: (805) 648-3197

Edoardo D'Antona
Via Monte Santo, 12
Rome 00195 Italy
Tel: (39) 6-560-0226
Fax: (39) 6-560-0226

Todd Eberle
54 West 21st Street #901
New York, New York 10010
Tel: (212) 243-2511
Fax: (212) 243-3587

Everett & Soulé, Orlando
  Skip Everett
  Anne Soulé
P.O. Box 150674
Altamonte Springs, Florida 32715
Tel: (407) 831-4183
Fax: (407) 831-4183

Galleria "Sul Po"
  Manuela Cerri
Via Andorno 22
Turin 10125 Italy
Tel: (39) 2-817-0738
Fax: (39) 2-812-5403

Housel Photo
  J.F. Housel
2307 Shoreland Drive
Seattle, Washington 98144
Tel: (206) 725-8442
Fax: (206) 725-8486

Jeff Garland Photography
  Jeff Garland
36304 Park Place Drive
Sterling Heights, Michigan 48310
Tel: (810) 264-4441
Fax: (810) 268-3289

Jennifer Lévy Photography
  Jennifer Lévy
245 West 29th Street
New York, New York 10001
Tel: (212) 465-8684
Fax: (212) 564-8083

John Sutton Photography
  John Sutton
8 Main Street
Point San Quentin, California 94964
Tel: (415) 258-8100
Fax: (415) 258-8167

David Livingston
1036 Erica Road
Mill Valley, California 94941
Tel: (415) 383-0898
Fax: (415) 383-0897

Mark Bolton Photography
  Mark Bolton
24 Bellevue Crescent
Bristol B58 4TE England
Tel: (44) 117-926-0867
Fax: (44) 117-926-0867

Michael E. Garland Photography
  Michael E. Garland
26 Avenue 28
Venice, California 90291
Tel: (310) 827-0670
Fax: (310) 285-1580

James Mortimer
15 Printing House Yard
Hackney Road
London E2 7NX England
Tel: (44) 171-729-8858

NRW Photography
  Nancy Robinson Watson
609 Ocean Drive #7H
Key Biscayne, Florida 33149
Tel: (305) 361-9182
Fax: (305) 361-6791

Phillip Ennis Photography
  Phillip Ennis
114 Millertown Road
Bedford, New York 10506
Tel: (914) 234-9574
Fax: (914) 234-0360

Eduardo Pozella
Rua Prof. José Leite e Oiticica, 137
Brooklin São Paulo, S.P. 04705-080
Brazil
Tel: (55) 11-534-5435
Fax: (55) 11-611-025

Randy G Photography
  Randy G
1008 South Washington #4
Royal Oak, Michigan 48067
Tel: (248) 399-2379
Fax: (248) 399-1026

Derek Rath
4044 Moore Street
Los Angeles, California 90066
Tel: (310) 305-1342
Fax: (310) 305-1342

Ray Allbright Photography
  Raymond Allbright
1799 Buckridge
Oro Vally, Arizona 85737
Tel: (502) 544-9128

Robert Thien Photography
  Robert Thien
2432 Sunset Drive
Atlanta, Georgia 30345
Tel: (404) 486-9813
Fax: (404) 486-9117

Sam Gray Photographer
  Sam Gray
23 Westwood Road
Wellesley, Massachusetts 02181
Tel: (617) 482-2246
Fax: (617) 482-1844

Samu Studios
  Mark Samu
P.O. Box 165
Bayport, New York 11705
Tel: (516) 363-5902
Fax: (516) 363-5242

Tim Lee Photography
  Tim Lee
2 Zachary Lane
New Milford, Connecticut 06776
Tel: (860) 355-4661
Fax: (860) 350-3526

Tom Bonner Photography
  Tom Bonner
1010 Abbott Kinney
Venice, California 90291
Tel: (310) 396-7125
Fax: (310) 396-4792

Tuca Reinés Estudio Foto Ltdo
  Tuca Reinés
Rua Emanuel Kant 58
São Paulo, S.P. 04536-050 Brazil
Tel: (55) 11-306-19127
Fax: (55) 11-852-8735

Will Brewster Photographer
  Will Brewster
Dry Fork Ranch
7823 Spring Hill Community Road
Belgrade, Montana 59714
Tel: (406) 587-5619
Fax: (406) 587-5619

Vicente Wolf Associates, Inc.
  Vicente Wolf
333 West 39th Street
New York, New York 10018
Tel: (212) 465-0590
Fax: (212) 465-0639

INDEX

175